THE AVENGERS

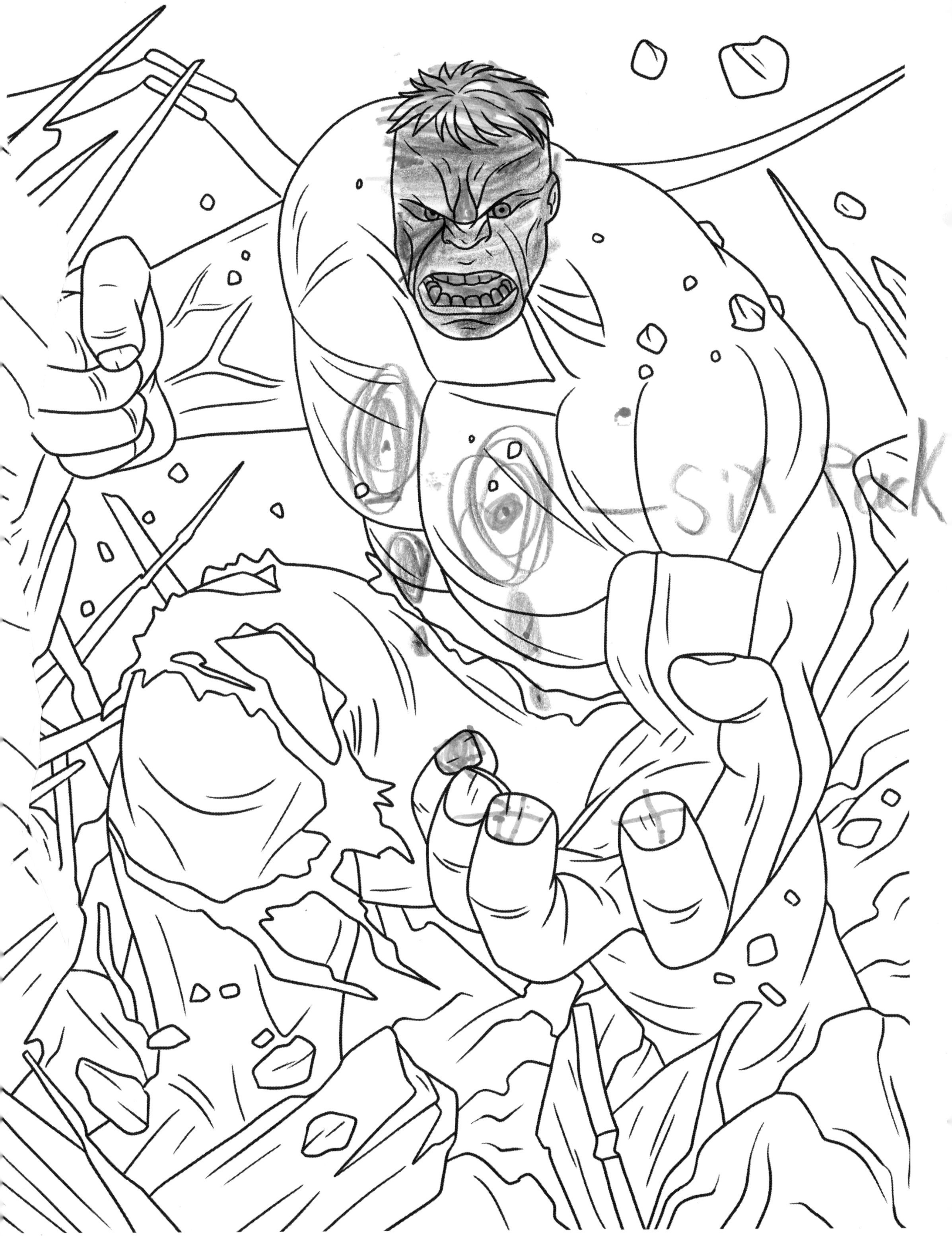
six Pack

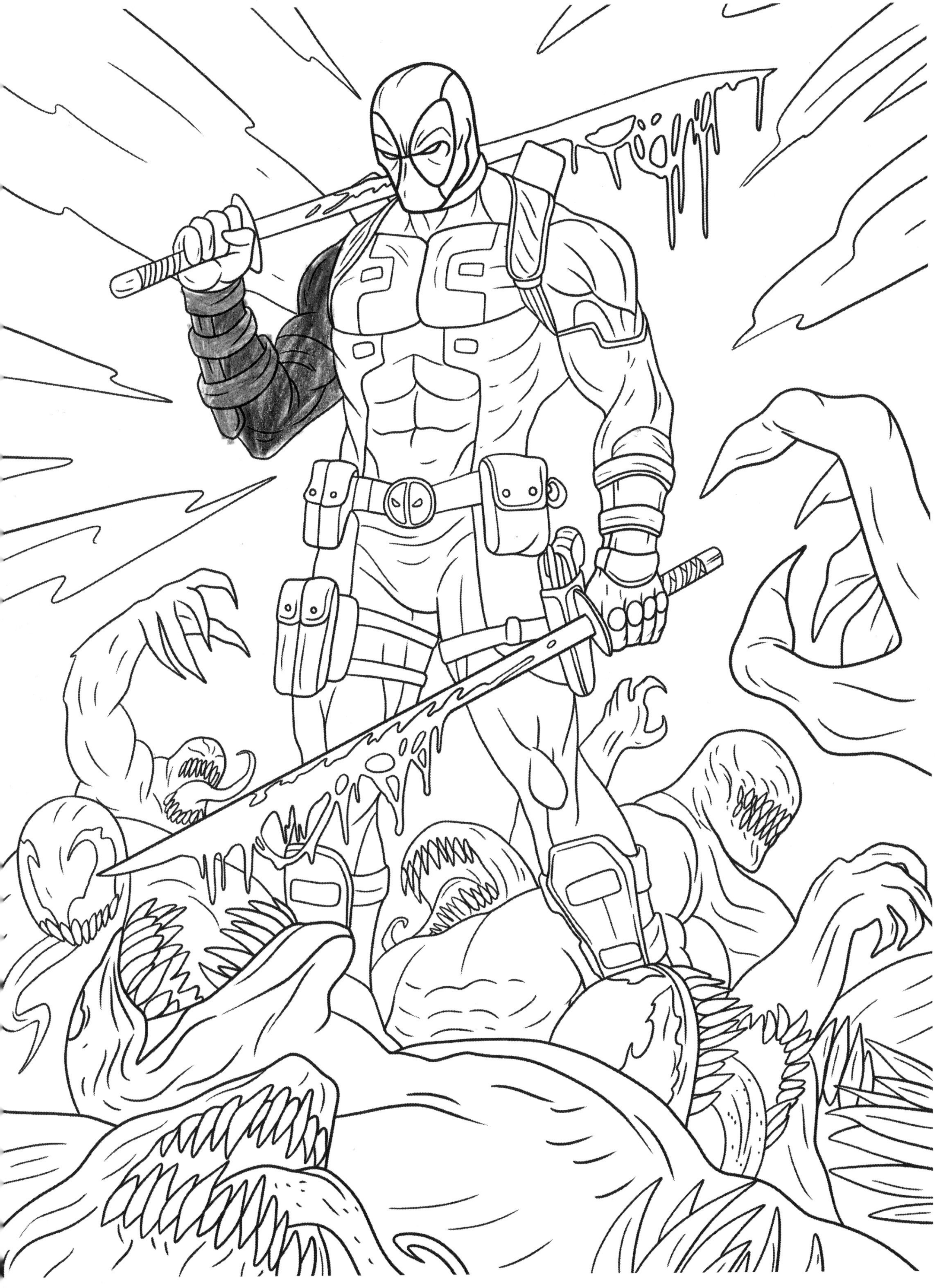

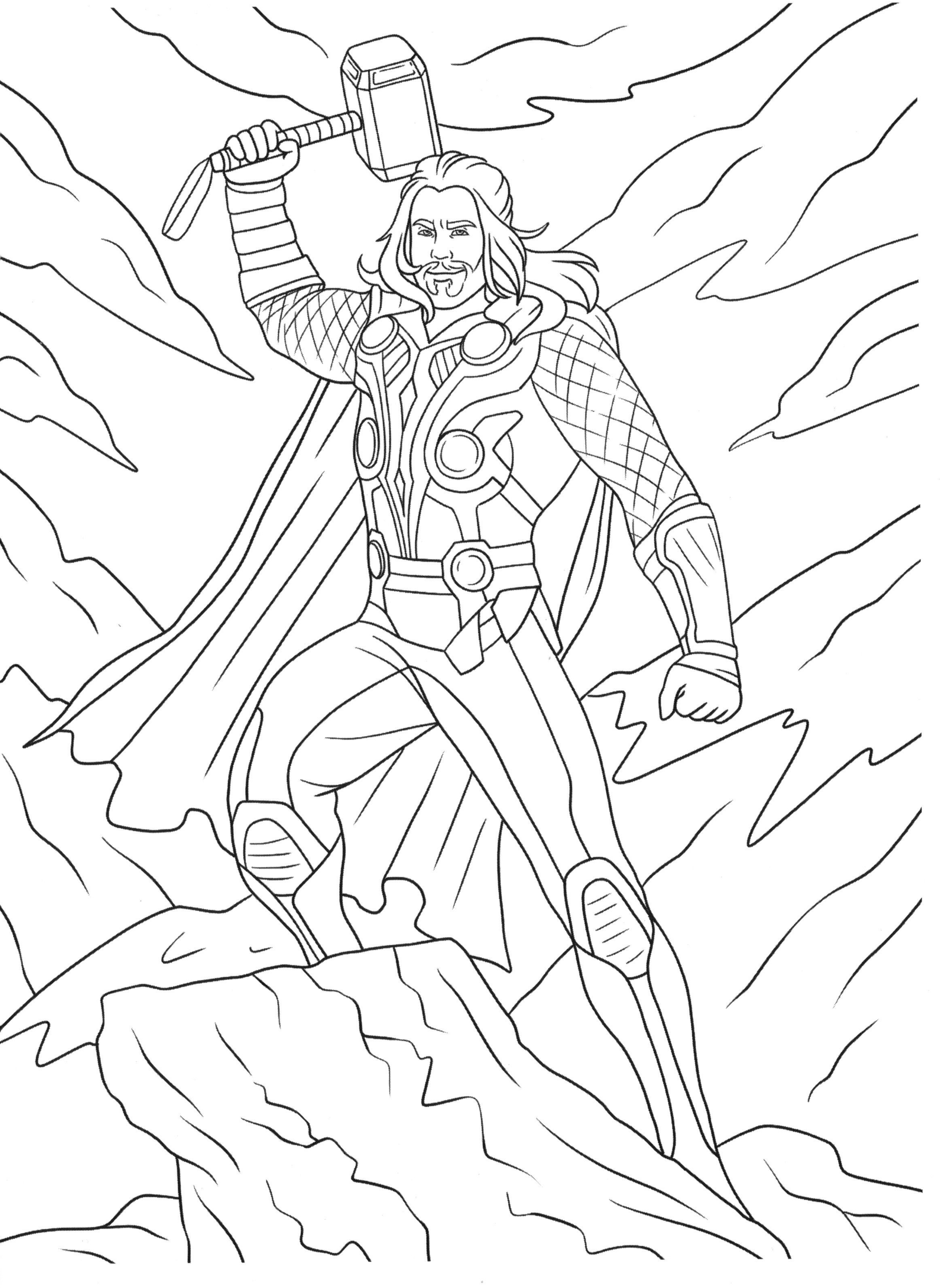

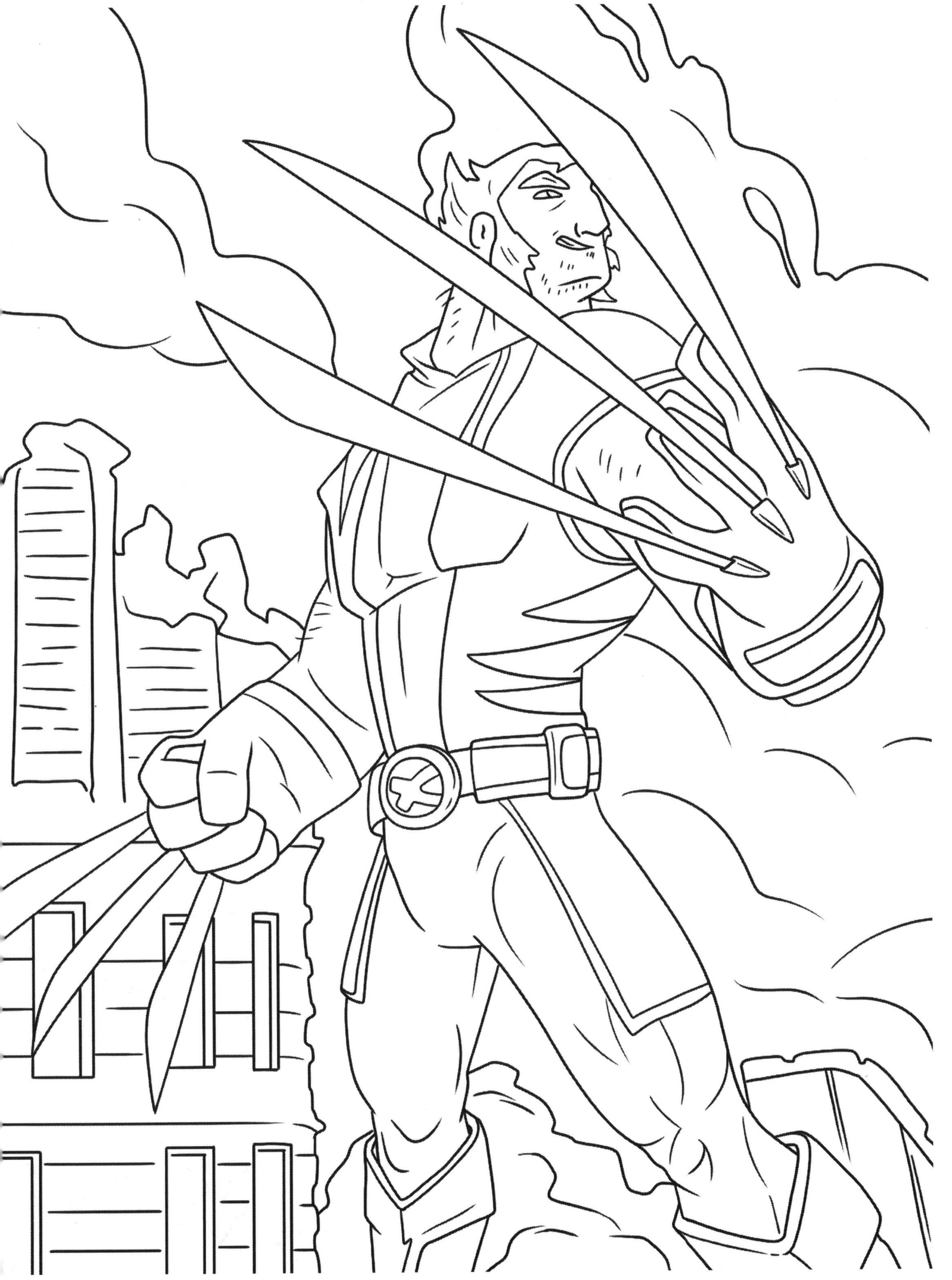

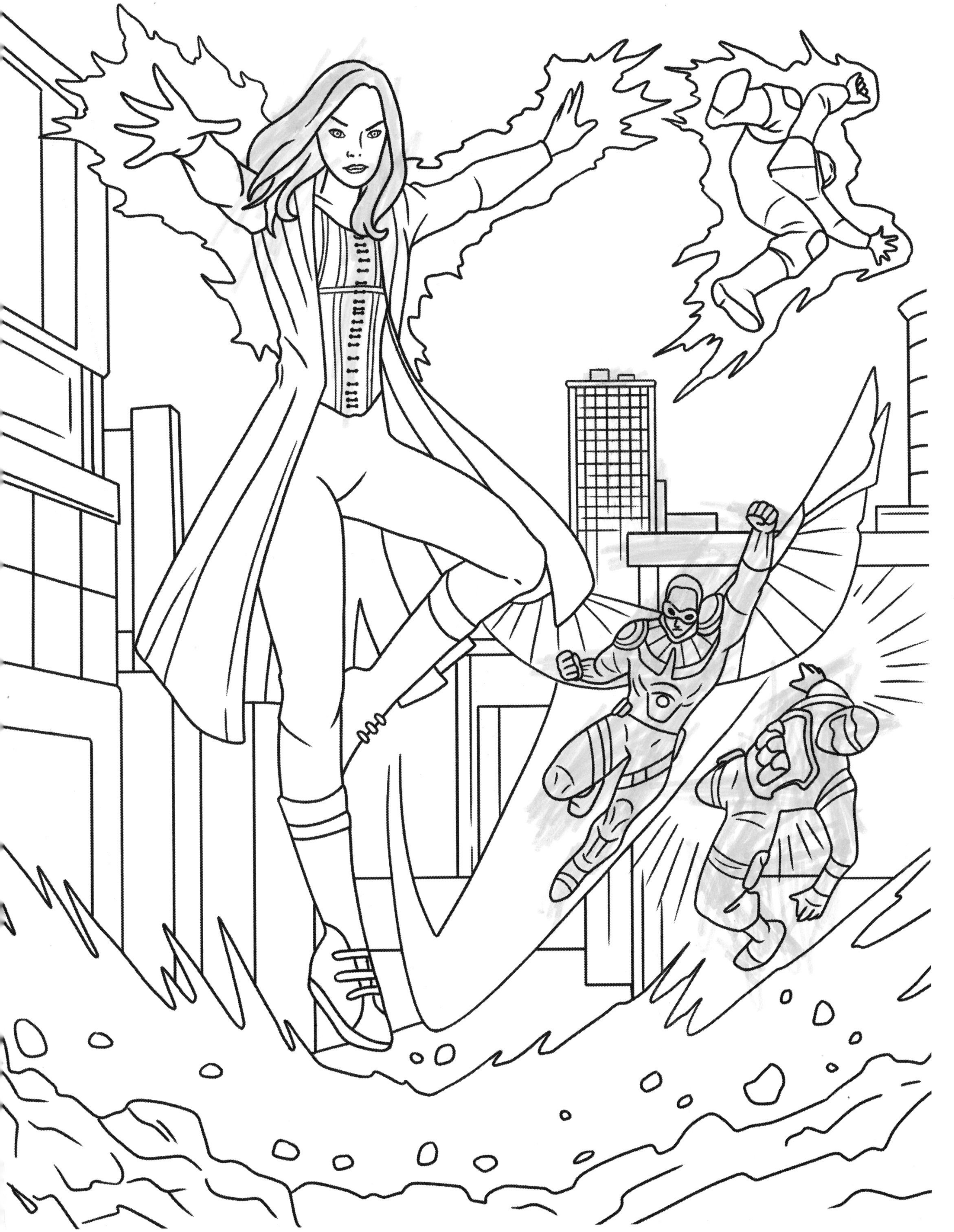

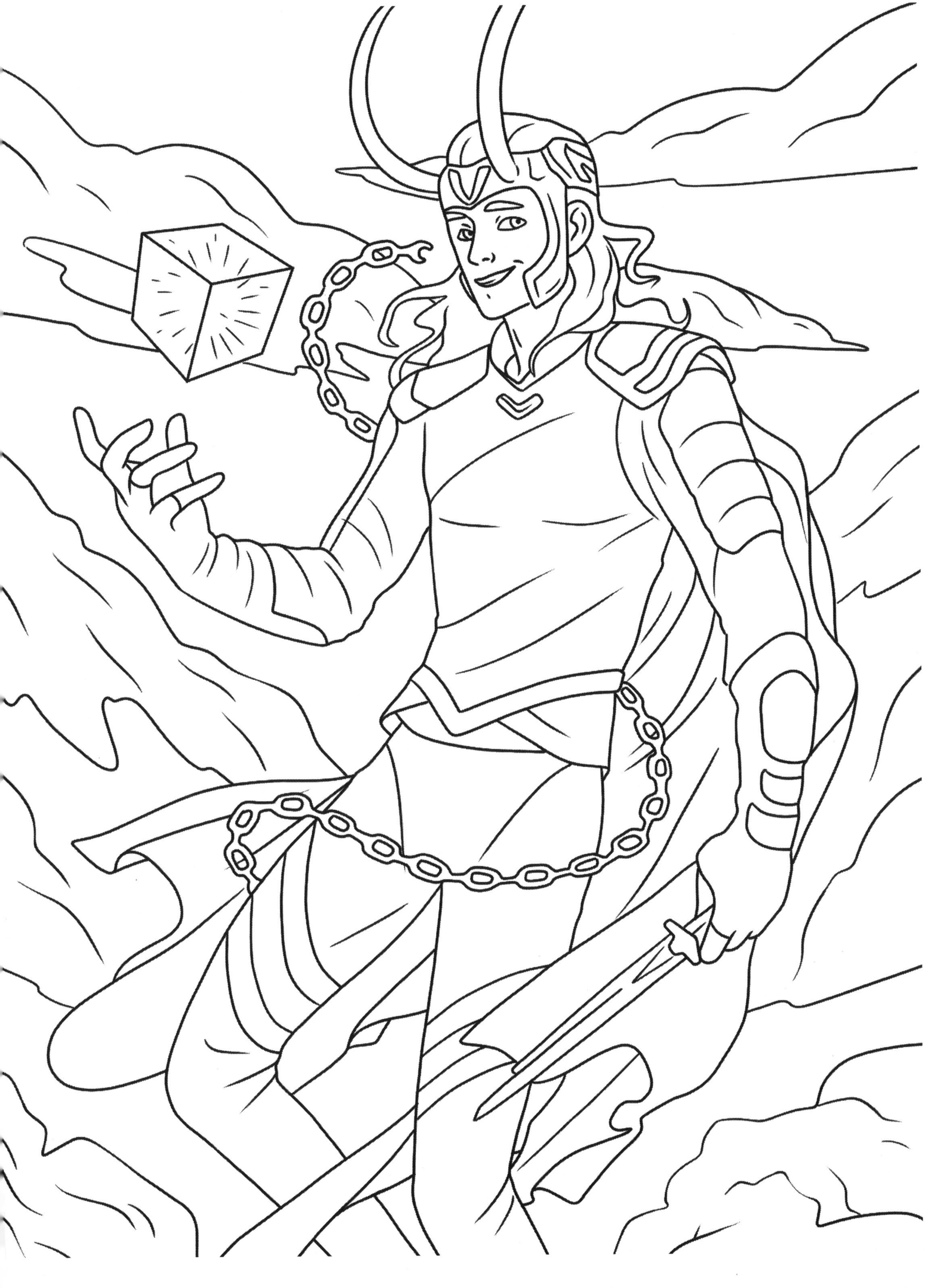

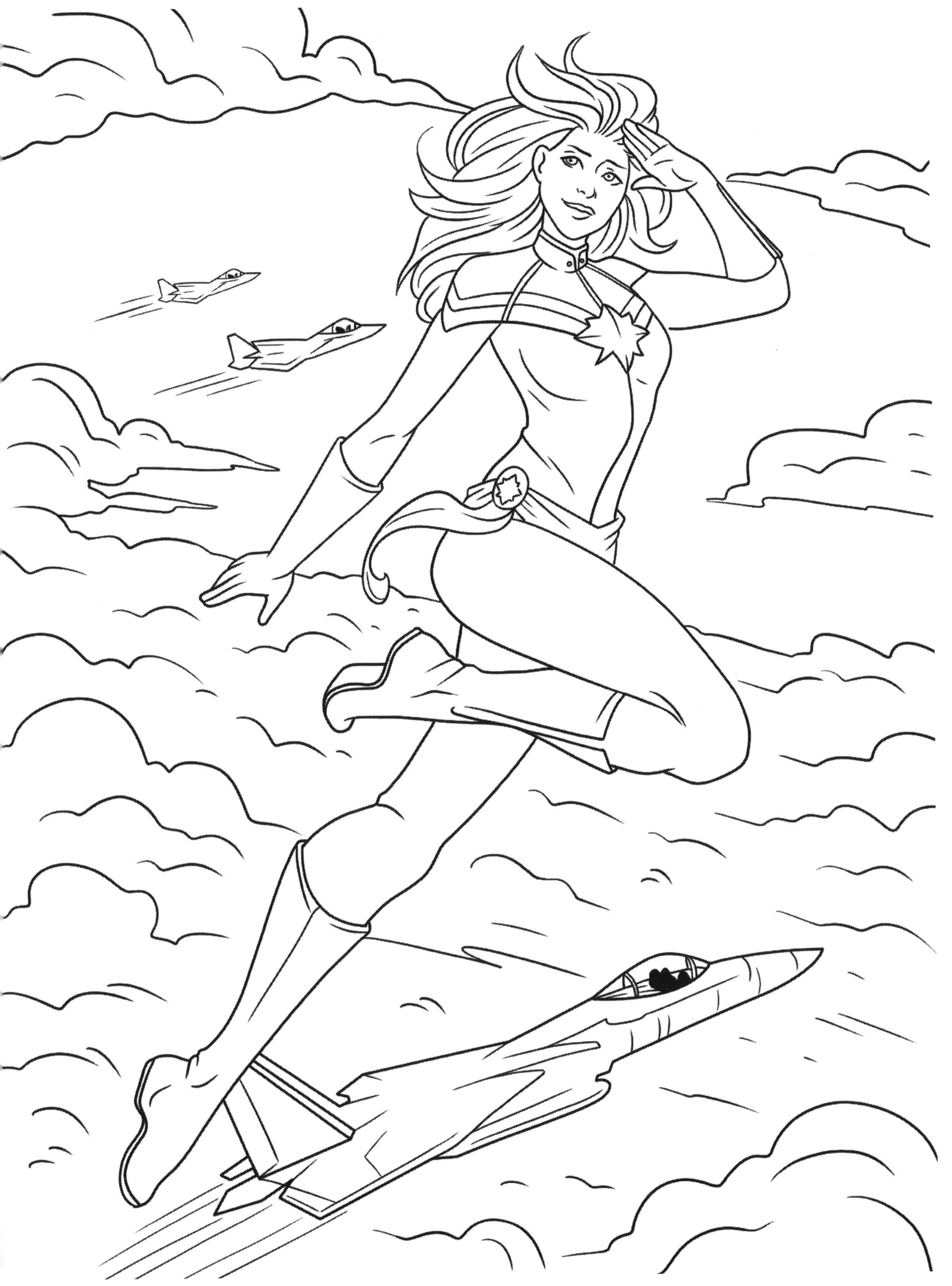

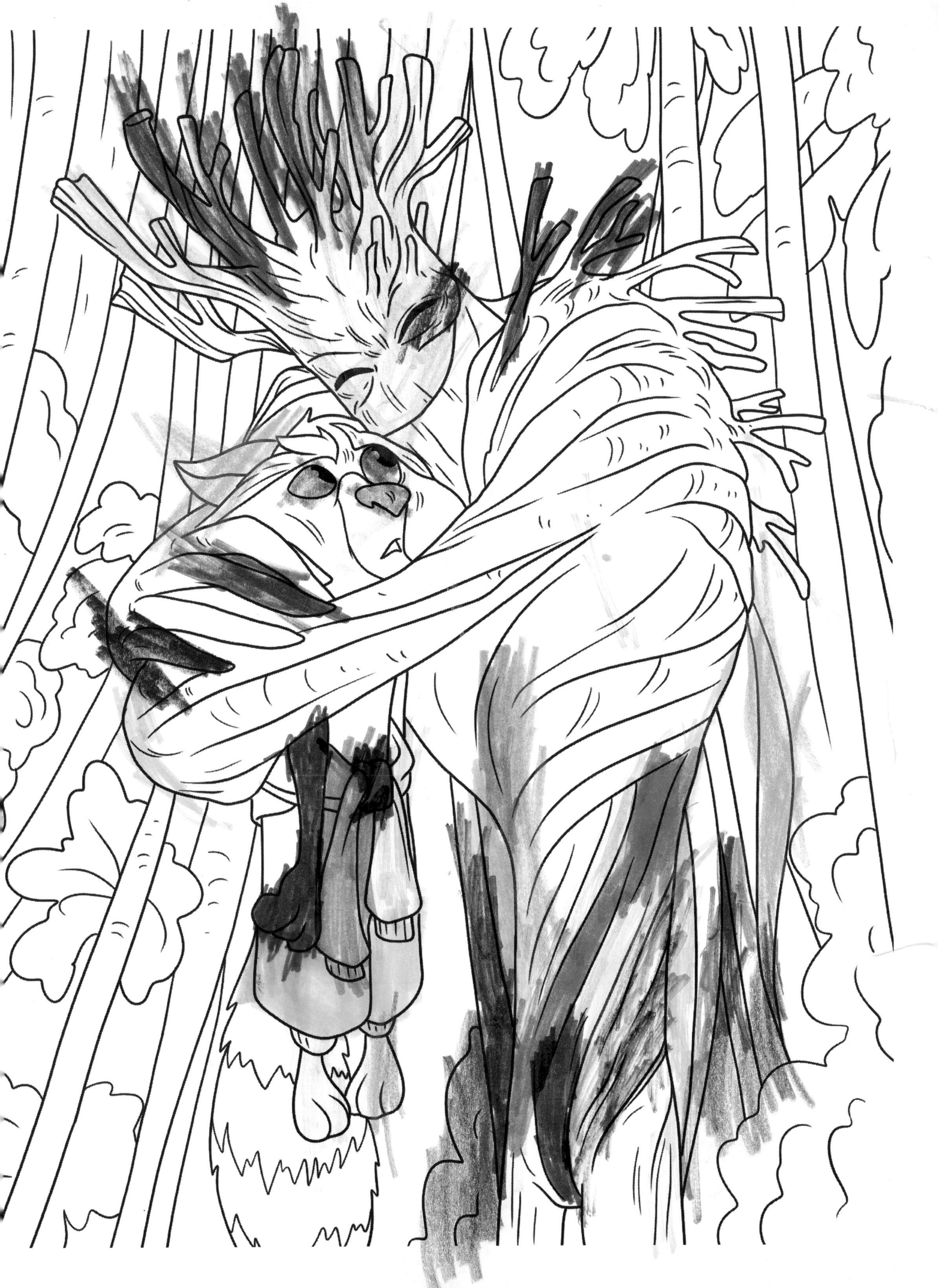

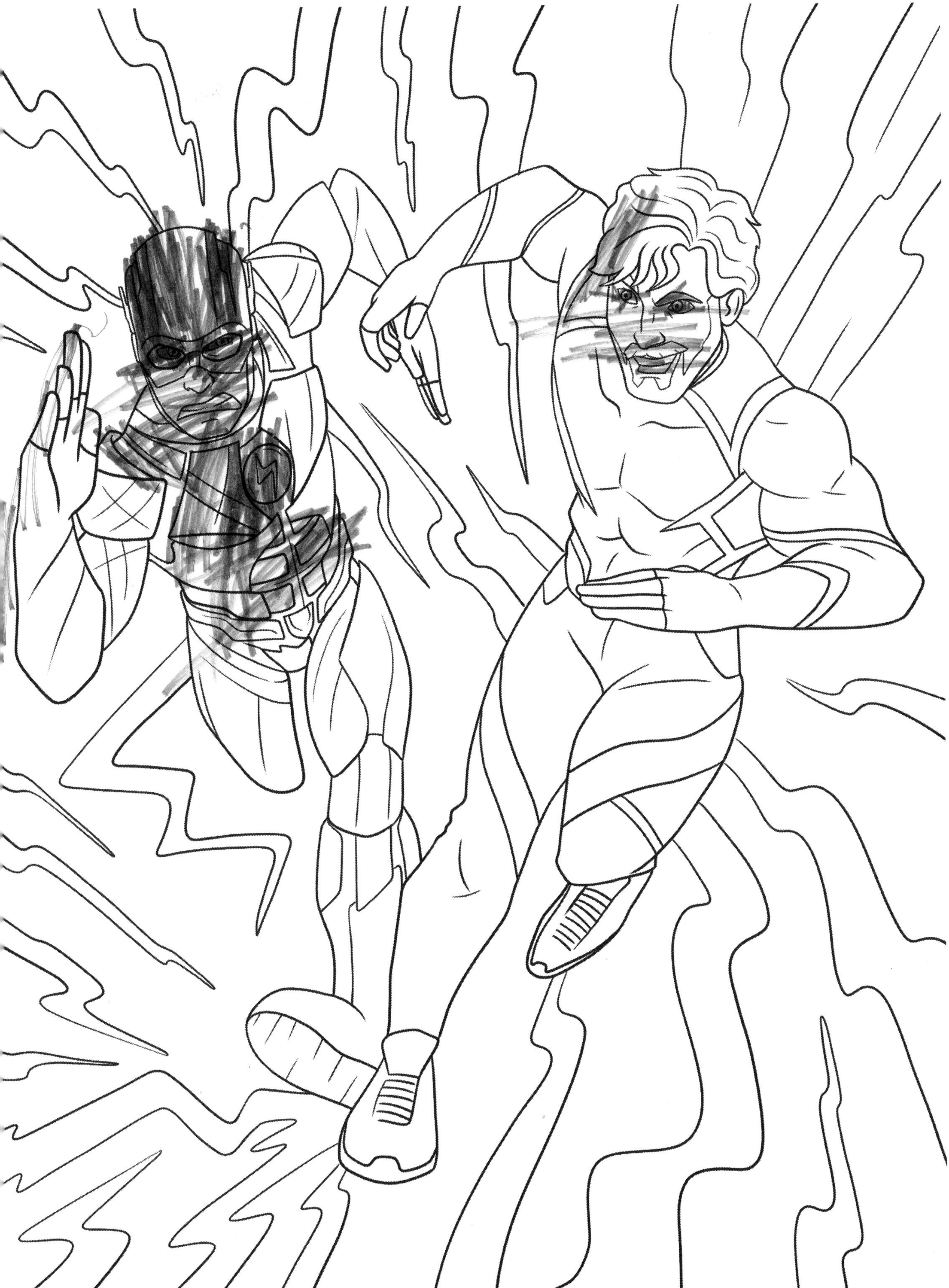

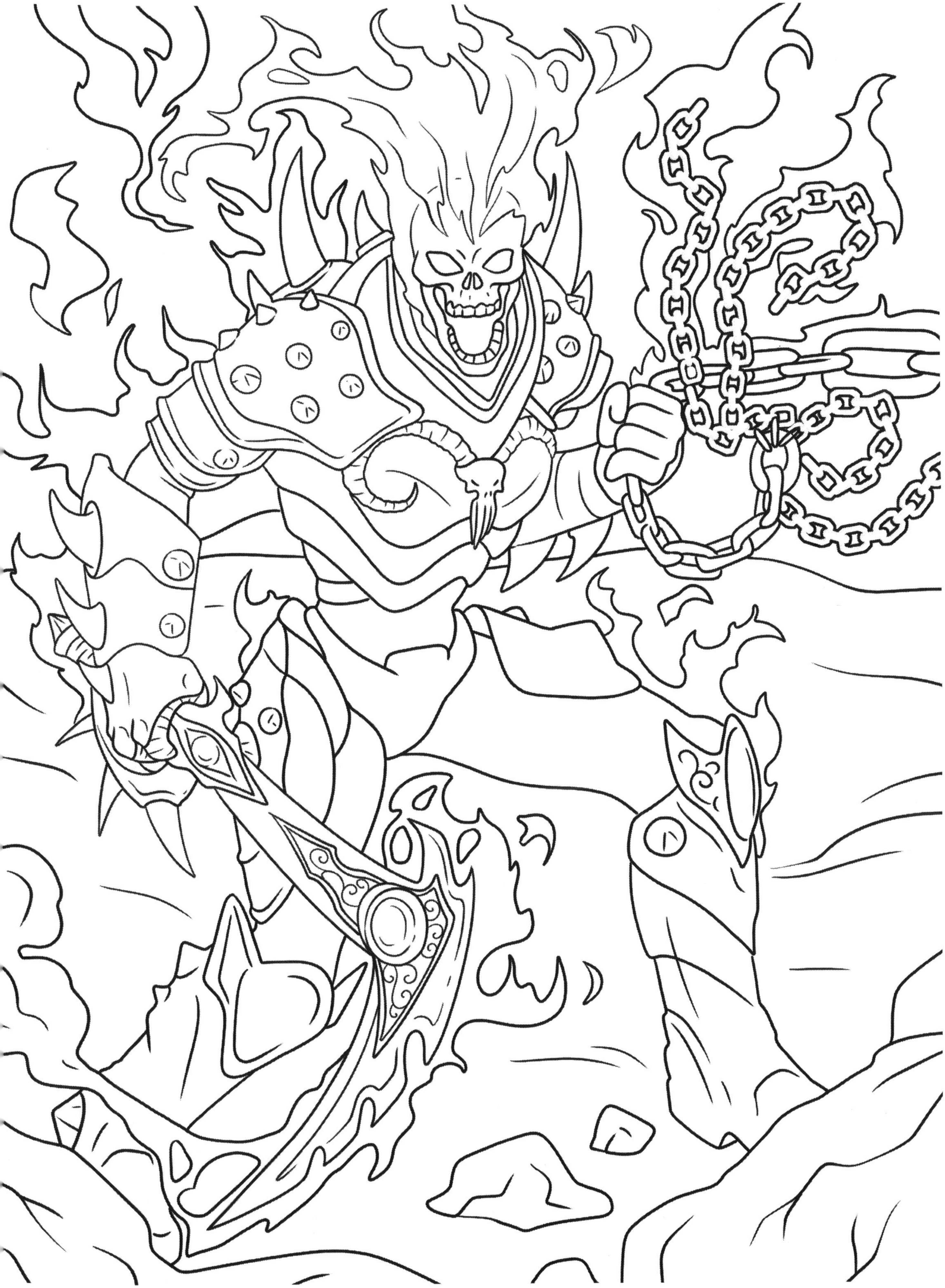

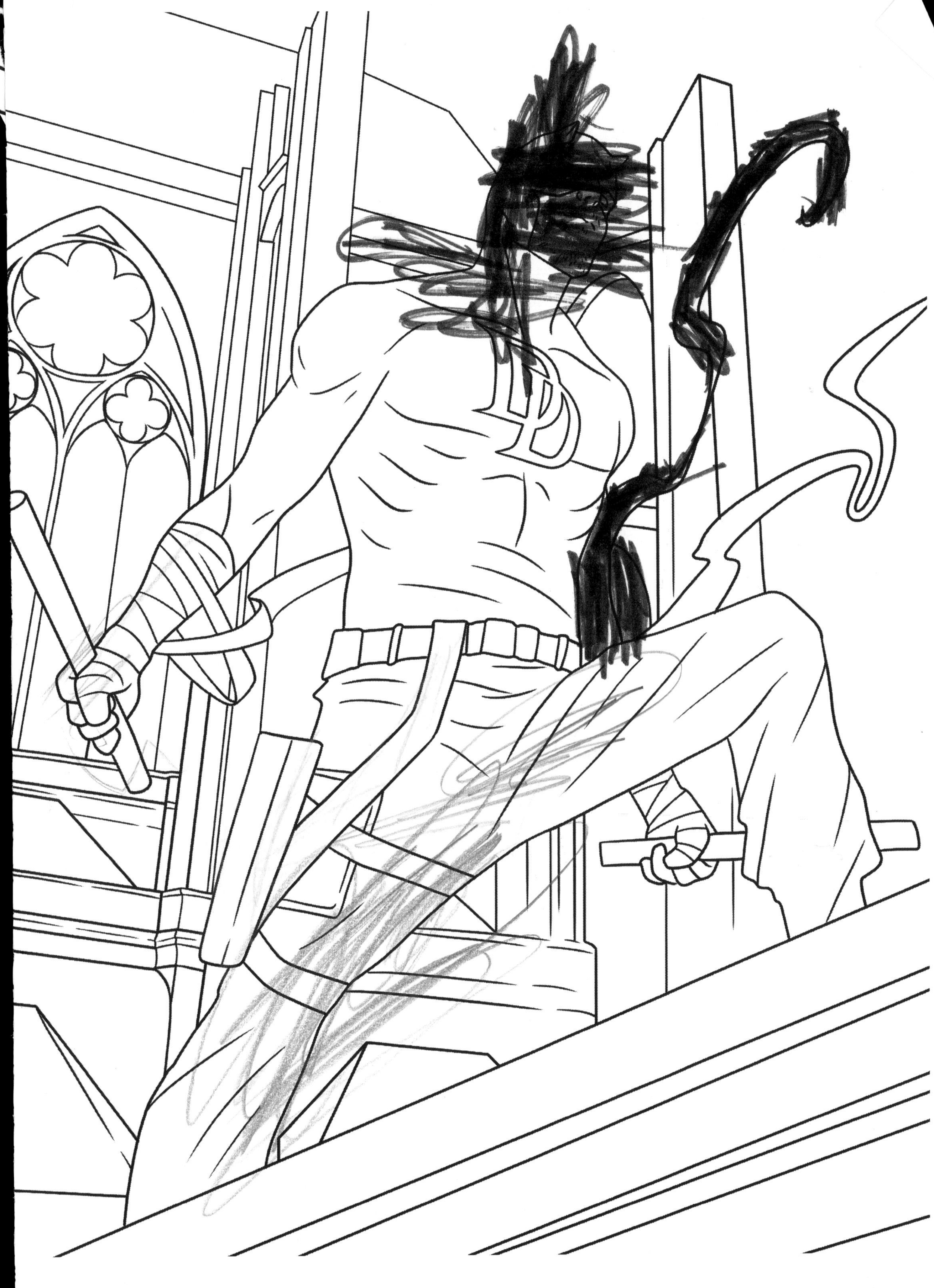

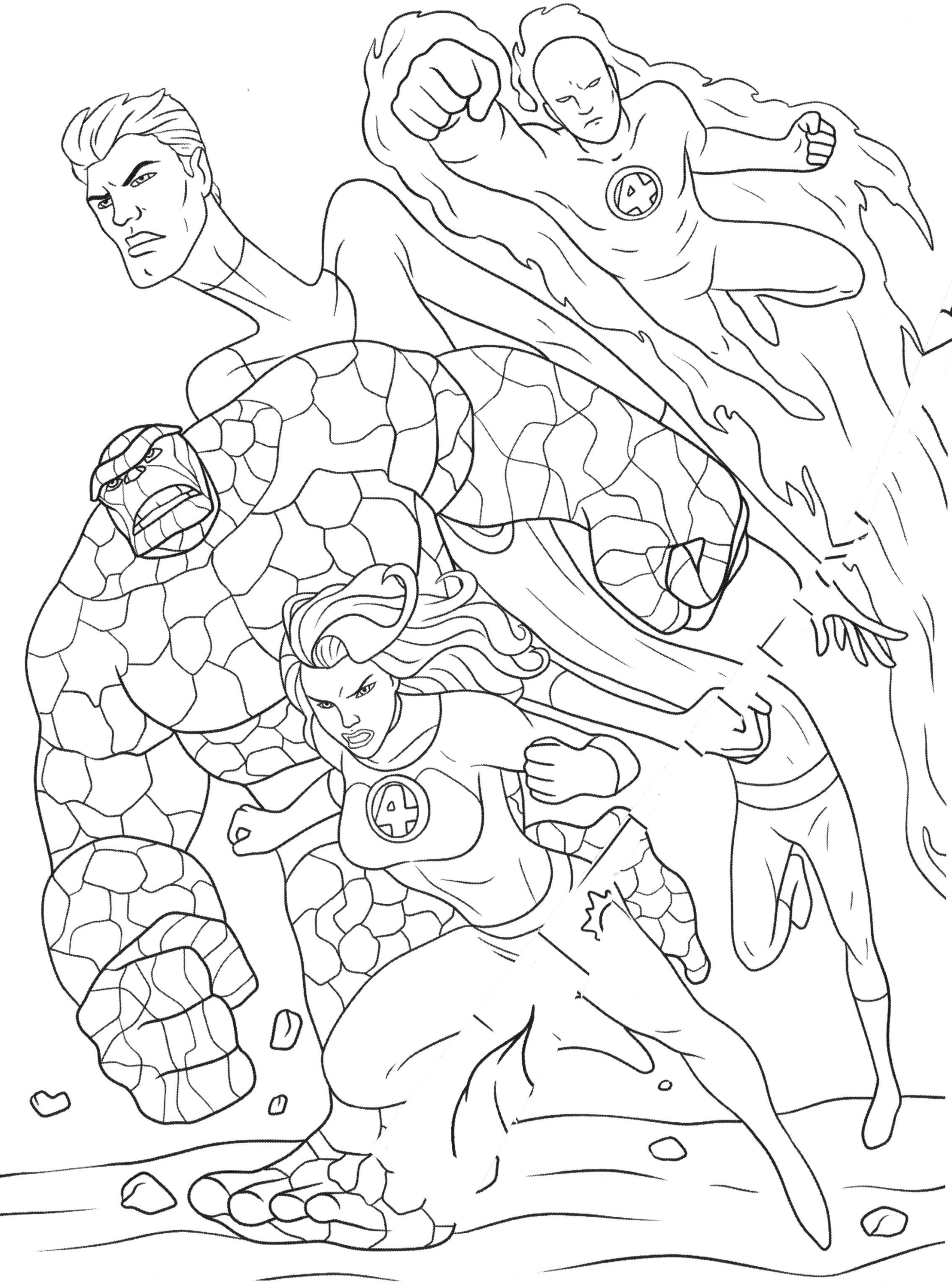

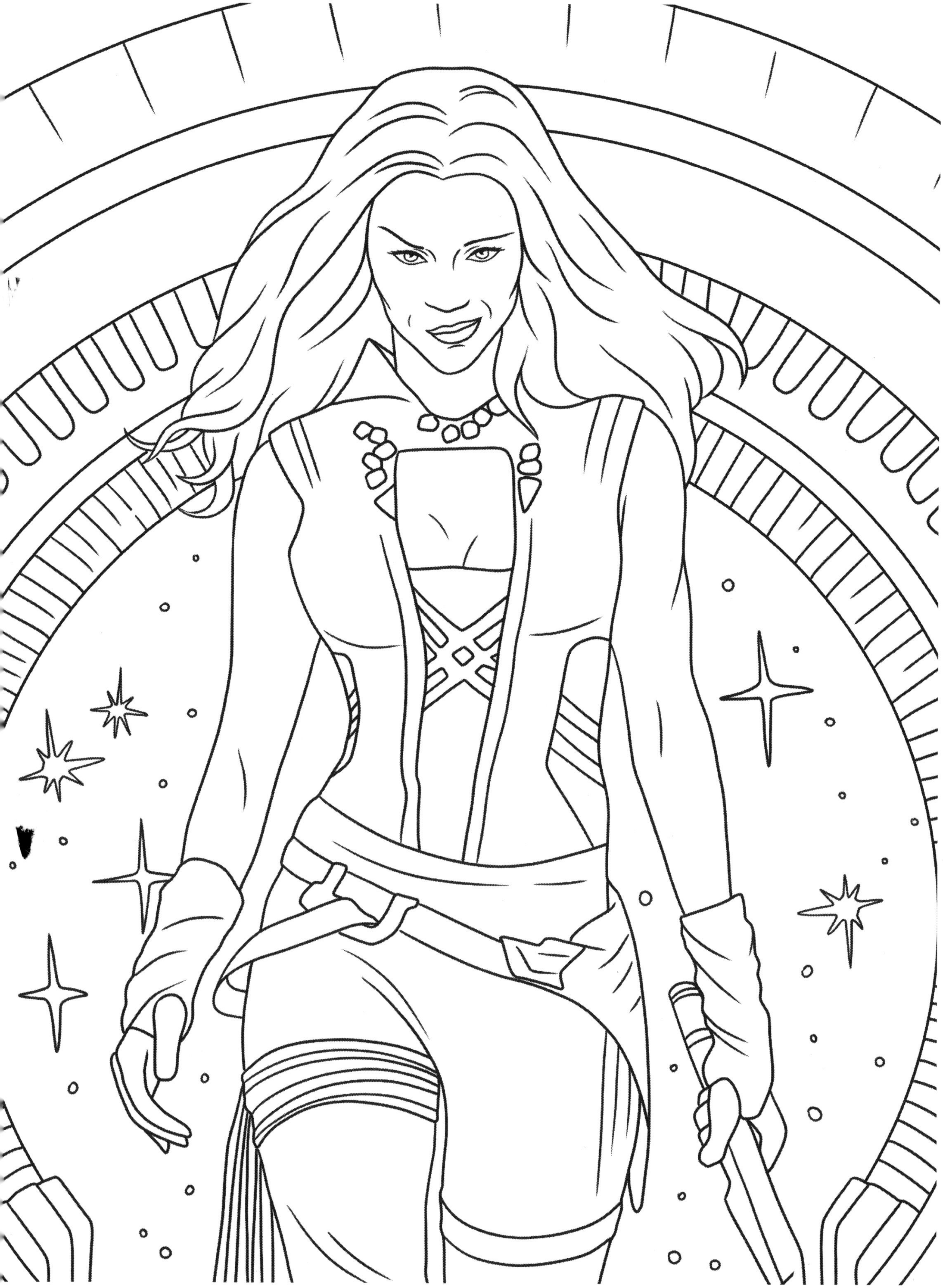

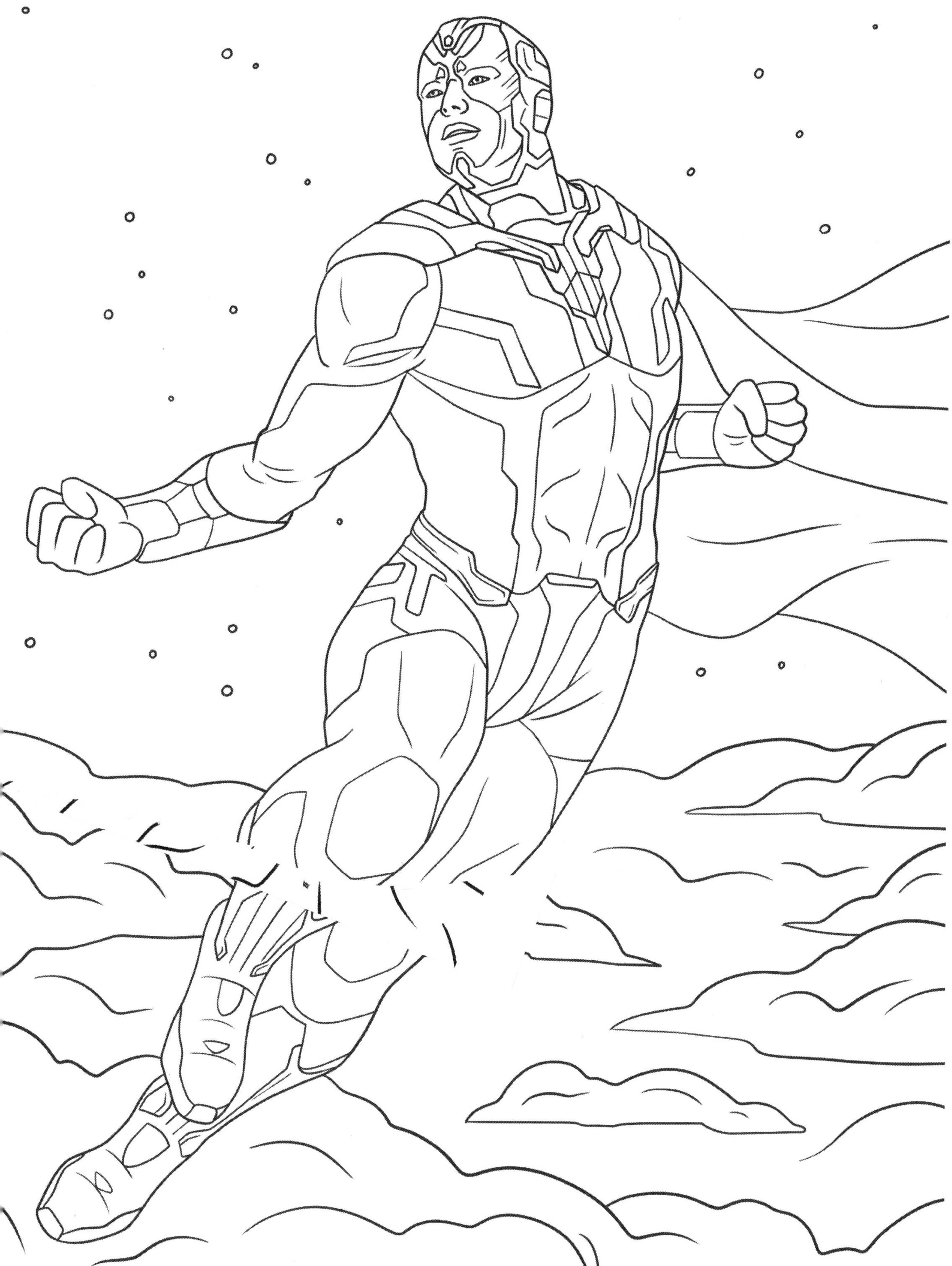

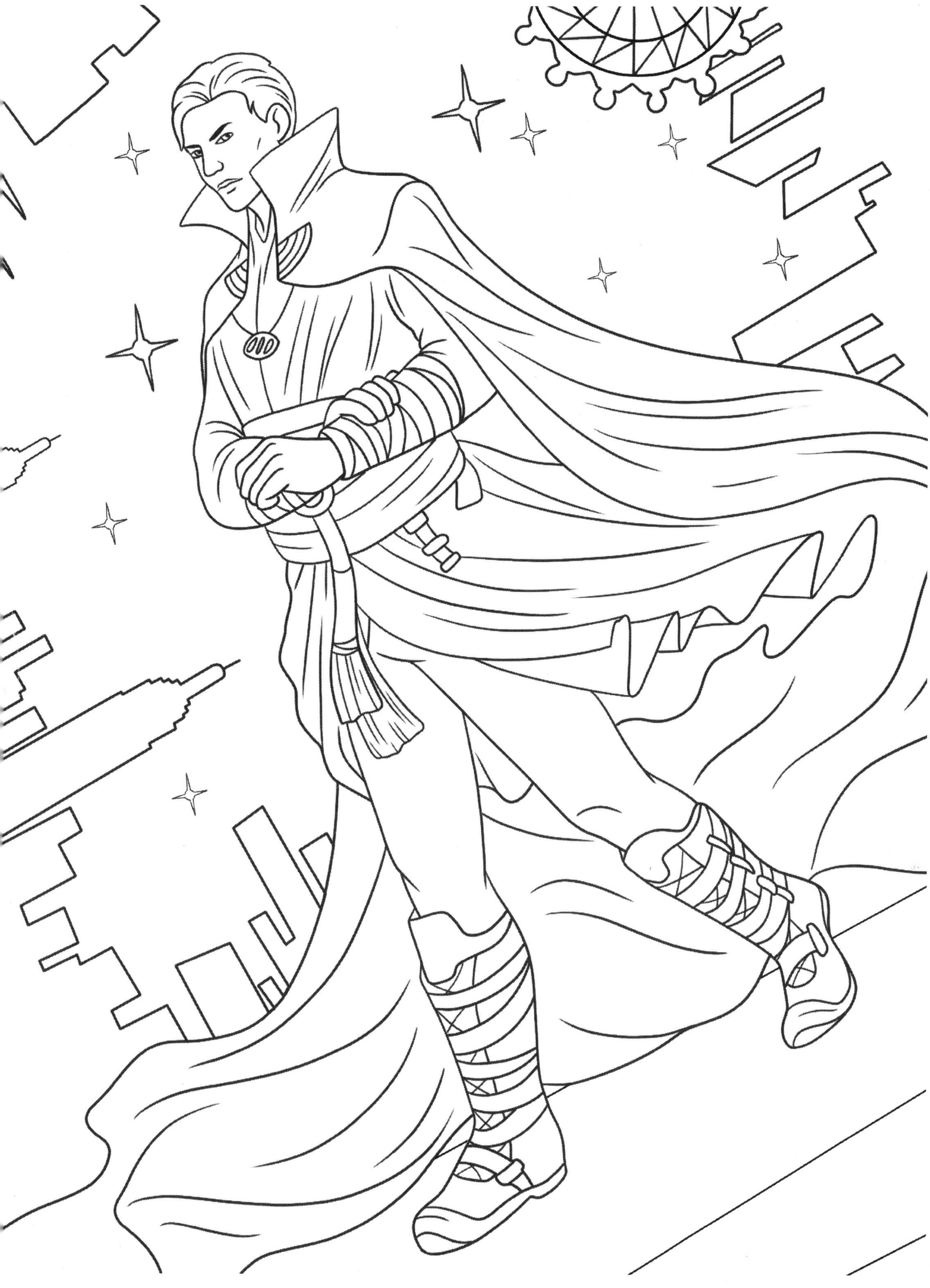

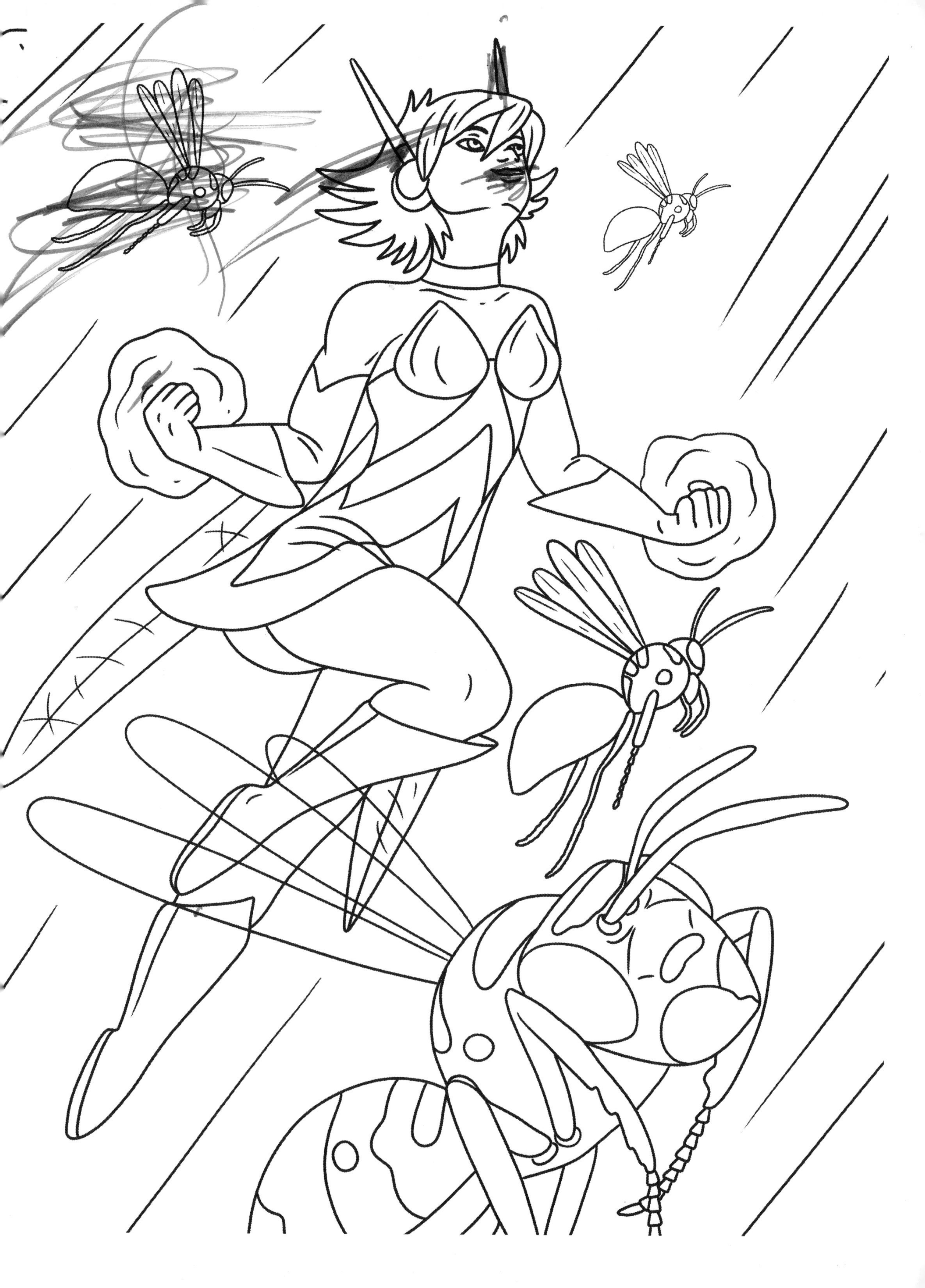

If you like the coloring book give us your feedback please